Beginning Biographies

Barack Obama
First African American President

Katie Kawa

PowerKiDS press™

NEW YORK

Published in 2013 by The Rosen Publishing Group, Inc.
29 East 21st Street, New York, NY 10010

Book Design: Katelyn Londino

Photo Credits: Cover (Obama) Feng Li/Staff/Getty Images News/Getty Images; cover (flag) Brandon Seidel/Shutterstock.com; p. 4 Christopher Halloran/
Shutterstock.com; pp. 5, 6, 7, 8, 11 Associated Press; p. 9 Laura S. L. Kong/Contributor/Hulton Archive/Getty Images; p. 10 Boston Globe/Contributor/Boston
Globe/Getty Images; p. 12 SAUL LOEB/Staff/AFP/Getty Images; p. 13 Solaria/Shutterstock.com; p. 14 Stephen C./Shutterstock.com; p. 15 Evan Meyer/
Shutterstock.com; p. 16 Alan Freed/Shutterstock.com; p. 17 JEWEL SAMAD/Staff/AFP/Getty Images; p. 18
commons.wikimedia.org/wiki/File:US_President_Barack_Obama_taking_his_Oath_of_Office_-_2009Jan20.jpg/wikipedia.org; p. 19 Handout/Handout/
Getty Images News/Getty Images; p. 20 The White House/Handout/Getty Images News/Getty Images; p. 21 MANDEL NGAN/Staff/AFP/Getty Images.

Library of Congress Cataloging-in-Publication Data

Kawa, Katie.
Barack Obama : first African American president / Katie Kawa.
     p. cm. — (Beginning biographies)
Includes index.
ISBN: 978-1-4488-8845-0
6-pack ISBN: 978-1-4488-8846-7
ISBN: 978-1-4488-8595-4 (library binding)
1. Obama, Barack—Juvenile literature. 2. Presidents—United States—Biography—Juvenile literature. 3. Racially mixed
people—United States—Biography—Juvenile literature. I. Title.
E908.K39 2013
973.932092—dc23
[B]
                                    2012012054

Manufactured in the United States of America

CPSIA Compliance Information: Batch #WS12RC: For further information contact Rosen Publishing, New York, New York at 1-800-237-9932.

Word Count: 426

Contents

An Important Leader

Barack Obama is the first African American person to be **elected** President of the United States. He's our 44th president.

Early Life

Barack was born in Hawaii on August 4, 1961.

He was named after his father, Barack Obama Sr.

Barack's father was from Kenya. Kenya is a country in east Africa. His mother was from Kansas. When Barack was growing up, he lived with his mom and not with his dad.

Barack's grandparents lived in Hawaii, too.

They helped raise him. His grandfather had served

in the army. His grandmother worked at a bank.

Barack lived in different places while he was growing up. He lived in a country in Asia called Indonesia. He learned about different kinds of people while living in Indonesia.

High School and College

Barack went to high school in Hawaii. He played basketball for his school's team. In 1979, he finished high school and started **college**.

Barack loved to learn about law. He went to a special college to study law. In 1991, he finished law school.

At Home in Chicago

Barack got a job as a teacher in Illinois. He taught law in the city of Chicago. He also wrote a book. It's called *Dreams from My Father*.

Barack's wife worked in Chicago, too. Her name is Michelle. She was a **lawyer**. Barack and Michelle got married in October 1992.

Making Laws

Barack wanted to help people in Illinois. He was elected to the Illinois **Senate** in 1996. He helped make laws for the state.

Barack worked in the Illinois Senate for many years.

Then, he was elected to the U.S. Senate

in November 2004.

Barack worked hard in the U.S. Senate. He helped make laws for everyone in America. This is an important job.

Running for President

In 2008, Barack ran for president. He gave **speeches** to get people to **vote** for him. His speeches made people feel that good things were ahead.

On November 4, 2008, Americans voted for their next president. This day is called Election Day. They picked Barack to be the president!

Life in the White House

Barack started his job as president on January 20, 2009. He and Michelle moved into the White House in Washington, D.C.

As the president's wife, Michelle is called the First Lady. Their two daughters live in the White House, too. Their names are Malia and Sasha. Michelle's mom also lives with them.

A president's life is very busy! Barack has many people who help him lead the country. He works with Congress to make laws for the country.

Working Hard

Barack Obama worked very hard to become president. Would you like to be the president when you grow up?

Barack Obama's Life

Barack is born in Hawaii.

Barack is elected to the state senate in Illinois.

Barack runs for president and wins.

1961

1996

2008

1979

2004

Barack finishes high school and starts college.

Barack is elected to the U.S. Senate.

Glossary

college (KAH-lihj) A school after high school.

elect (ih-LEHKT) To choose by voting.

lawyer (LOY-uhr) A person whose job is to practice law.

senate (SEHN-eht) A group that makes laws.

speech (SPEECH) A public talk.

vote (VOHT) To tell or show which one you would like.

Index

Due to the changing nature of Internet links, The Rosen Publishing Group, Inc., has developed an online list of websites related to the subject of this book. This site is updated regularly. Please use this link to access the list: **www.powerkidslinks.com/bbio/obama**